Sports Illustrated KIDS
STARS OF SPORTS

JOEL EMBIID

BASKETBALL STAR SHOOTER

by Cheryl Kim

CAPSTONE PRESS
a capstone imprint

Published by Capstone Press, an imprint of Capstone
1710 Roe Crest Drive, North Mankato, Minnesota 56003
capstonepub.com

Library of Congress Cataloging-in-Publication Data
Names: Kim, Cheryl, author.
Title: Joel Embiid : basketball star shooter / By Cheryl Kim.
Description: North Mankato, Minnesota : Capstone Press, [2023] | Series: Sports illustrated kids stars of sports | Includes bibliographical references and index. | Audience: Ages 8-11 | Audience: Grades 4-6 | Summary: "Joel Embiid started playing basketball in his home country of Cameroon at age 15. He soon moved to the U.S. to play basketball and went on to become a star high school player. Embiid made his NBA debut in 2016 and was named to the All-Star Game in 2018. That same year, he became one of just seven players with 2,000 points, 1,000 rebounds, and 200 blocks in his first 100 games. Discover how Embiid overcame injuries to become one of the NBA's brightest stars"-- Provided by publisher.
Identifiers: LCCN 2022005385 (print) | LCCN 2022005386 (ebook) | ISBN 9781666347333 (hardcover) | ISBN 9781666347340 (pdf) | ISBN 9781666347364 (kindle edition)
Subjects: LCSH: Embiid, Joel, 1994---Juvenile literature. | Basketball players--Cameroon--Biography--Juvenile literature. | Centers (Basketball)--United States--Biography--Juvenile literature.
Classification: LCC GV884.E52 K56 2023 (print) | LCC GV884.E52 (ebook) | DDC 796.323092 [B]--dc23
LC record available at https://lccn.loc.gov/2022005385
LC ebook record available at https://lccn.loc.gov/2022005386

Editorial Credits
Editor: Carrie Sheely; Designer: Bobbie Nuytten; Media Researcher: Morgan Walters; Production Specialist: Polly Fisher

Image Credits
Associated Press: Chris Pizzello, 25, Chris Szagola, 5, Nick Wass, 24, Rebecca Blackwell, 11, Themba Hadebe, 27; Newscom: Rich Graessle, 13, Steven M. Falk/TNS, 17, Yong Kim/Philadelphia Daily News/TNS, 19; Shutterstock: Homo Cosmicos, 7, Vasyl Shulga, 1; Sports Illustrated: Al Tielemans, 9, David E. Klutho, 15, Erick W. Rasco, Cover, 8, 21, 23, 28

Source Notes
Pg. 4, "Having the fans . . . " "Joel Embiid Dazzles in Debut, Scoring 20 Points in Sixers Loss," ESPN, October 26, 2016, https://www.espn.com/nba/story/_/id/17897787/joel-embiid-philadelphia-76ers-scores-20-points-long-awaited-debut
Pg. 6, "The way they . . . " "NBA Star Joel Embiid Was So Bad at Basketball He Watched YouTube Videos to Improve—Here's How He Ultimately Found Success," CNBC, October 16, 2018, https://www.cnbc.com/2018/10/16/nba-star-joel-embiid-watched-youtube-videos-to-learn-how-to-shoot.html
Pg. 8, "I was so nervous . . . " Ibid.
Pg. 10, "I was kind of," "Meet the Man Who Discovered Joel Embiid and Pascal Siakam," Sportscasting, December 23, 2019, https://www.sportscasting.com/meet-the-man-who-discovered-joel-embiid-and-pascal-siakam/
Pg. 12, "I went back . . . " "It's Story Time," The Players' Tribune, August 31, 2018, https://www.theplayerstribune.com/articles/joel-embiid-its-story-time
Pg. 12, ". . . I'd just try . . . " "Joel Embiid First Learned How to Shoot a Basketball by Searching 'White People Shooting 3-Pointers' on YouTube," Sportscasting, May 21, 2021, https://www.sportscasting.com/joel-embiid-first-learned-shoot-basketball-searching-white-people-shooting-3-pointers-youtube/
Pg. 18, "I really just wanted . . . " "Joel Embiid Almost Quit Basketball After His Brother's Tragic Death," Sportscasting, August 19, 2020, https://www.sportscasting.com/joel-embiid-almost-quit-basketball-after-his-brothers-tragic-death/
Pg. 24, "This is where I . . . " "Joel Embiid Opens Up About Fatherhood, How His Son Is Motivating Him," NBC 10 Philadelphia, February 3, 2021, https://www.nbcphiladelphia.com/news/sports/sixers/joel-embiid-opens-up-about-fatherhood-how-his-son-is-motivating-him/2691039/?amp
Pg. 26, "Basketball has . . . " "NBA's Joel Embiid Breaks Stereotypes with Under Armour Endorsement Deal," Fashion Network, October 12, 2018, https://us.fashionnetwork.com/news/Nba-s-joel-embiid-breaks-stereotypes-with-under-armour-endorsement-deal,1023736.html

Printed and bound in the USA. PO4882

TABLE OF CONTENTS

Words in **BOLD** are in the glossary.

A LONG-AWAITED DEBUT

Joel Embiid stepped onto the court for his **debut** National Basketball Association (NBA) game. The crowd went wild. After missing two seasons because of foot injuries, Embiid received cheers each time he touched the ball. As Embiid stood at the free throw line, fans chanted, "Trust the process!" Scoring 20 points in the first 22 minutes, Embiid reminded people why he was the number three pick in the 2014 NBA **Draft**. "Having the fans chant that, it was special and I loved it," said Embiid.

Trust the Process

Former Philadelphia 76ers general manager Sam Hinkie talked about process. He used the word to describe the team's focus on giving up short-term wins for long-term victories. Eventually, the phrase "Trust the process" became popular with Philadelphia fans. It's now widely used in U.S. popular culture. "The Process" is also Embiid's nickname.

CHAPTER 1

DISCOVERED

Joel Hans Embiid was born on March 16, 1994, in Yaoundé, Cameroon. His parents are Thomas and Christine Embiid. Thomas was a military officer. He also played professional **handball**. Joel grew up with his brother, Arthur, and his sister, Muriel. Christine often helped Joel and his siblings with their schoolwork. She wanted Joel to become a doctor. But she also encouraged him to follow his dreams.

As a child, Embiid played volleyball and soccer. He wanted to play professional volleyball in Europe someday.

When he was 15, Embiid watched his first NBA game on TV. After seeing Kobe Bryant in the 2009 NBA Finals, Embiid's interest turned toward basketball. "The way they moved, and the athleticism, I thought it was the coolest thing in the world," said Embiid. "I had that moment like, 'I just wanna do that.'"

>>> Yaoundé, Cameroon

FACT

Cameroon is a country in west-central Africa.
Basketball is a popular sport there.

Embiid began playing basketball at a local court. When Embiid was 16, Cameroon native and NBA player Luc Mbah a Moute invited the then 6-foot-10-inch- (208-centimeter-) tall Embiid to a local basketball camp. "I was so nervous that I didn't even show up the first day," remembers Embiid. He didn't want to embarrass himself playing against more experienced athletes. But Embiid did go the next day. He made a dunk in a game and started gaining confidence.

〉〉〉 Embiid is known for making big dunks in the NBA.

Luc Mbah a Moute played in the NBA from 2008 to 2020.

Embiid's brief performance got him an invitation to the Basketball Without Borders program. The program allows players in many countries to develop their skills at camps. "I was kind of shy . . . [but] by the end of the weekend, I felt comfortable. . . . I ended up kind of showing my potential." At the end of the four-day camp, a private high school in Florida named Montverde Academy offered Embiid a basketball **scholarship**.

Basketball Without Borders

Basketball Without Borders (BWB) is the NBA and International Basketball Federation's (FIBA) global basketball development and community outreach program. It has held camps in 30 countries on six continents. It has reached more than 3,000 participants. More than 65 campers have been in the NBA. Embiid participates in the program in Africa to help young players.

>>> Participants in a Basketball Without Borders camp in Africa attend the opening press conference.

CHAPTER 2

PATH TO THE NBA

Embiid soon moved to the United States to join the junior varsity team at Montverde Academy. Some of his teammates made fun of him because he struggled with shooting. "I went back to my dorm room and cried," said Embiid. He thought about going back home. Then his competitive side kicked in. "I got really, really motivated. Whenever people say I can't do something, I actually love it. It makes me want to prove them wrong so bad," said Embiid.

Embiid worked hard to get better. He began working out with one of his teammates. He also searched for instructional videos. ". . . I'd just try to imitate how they shot the ball, and I started being able to compete." After practices, Embiid would stay in the gym for hours to do three-point drills and practice his shots.

>>> As one of the country's best high school basketball players, Embiid was invited to play in the Jordan Brand Classic in April 2013.

Embiid spent his senior year of high school playing for The Rock School in Gainesville, Florida. He helped lead his team to the **playoffs** and the state championship.

In late 2012, Embiid enrolled at the University of Kansas as a five-star recruit. These players are rated as the top 25 to 30 high school players in the country.

During his first practice game, a teammate dunked the ball on Embiid while he was defending near the rim. People watching the game started laughing. Embarrassed, Embiid asked his coach to delay starting him. His coach, Bill Self, believed in Embiid's talent. He said Embiid would soon be the number one NBA draft pick if he didn't give up. Embiid kept playing and was named the Big 12 Defensive Player of the Year. A back injury kept Embiid out of the NCAA and Big 12 tournaments.

>>> Embiid goes up for a shot during a game between the University of Kansas and Iowa State in 2014.

CHAPTER 3
TRUSTING THE PROCESS

In spring 2014, Embiid had a decision to make. He could be in the 2014 NBA Draft or plan on returning to college for the next season. Embiid decided to enter the draft. Despite his recent injury, the Philadelphia 76ers drafted him. Embiid told reporters and fans he was so excited but also in disbelief.

Embiid missed his first NBA season due to a foot injury. That year, Embiid's 13-year-old brother, Arthur, died. Although they were very close, Embiid hadn't seen Arthur since he left for America four years before. Embiid returned to Cameroon for the memorial service.

FACT

Embiid became the fourth draft pick from Cameroon in the NBA.

>>> After injuring his foot, Embiid had to focus on recovery.

The tragedy led Embiid to consider retiring from basketball before even playing in an NBA game. "I really just wanted to quit the game and go back home to Cameroon to be with my family," recalled Embiid. "Every single morning, when I woke up, I would tell myself that I had a choice. I could give up, or I could keep trying to take another step forward." Embiid decided to keep playing basketball.

Embiid's slow recovery and foot surgery kept him from playing again in the 2015–2016 season. Embiid returned in the 2016–2017 season for his first NBA game. He went on to average 20.2 points, 7.8 rebounds, and 2.1 **assists** per game that season. The Eastern Conference named Embiid **Rookie** of the Month for November and December of 2016 and again in January 2017. A knee injury kept Embiid out for the remainder of the season.

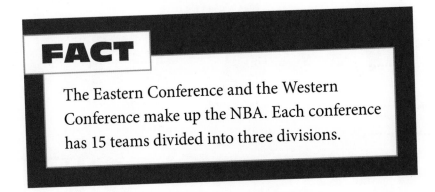

FACT

The Eastern Conference and the Western Conference make up the NBA. Each conference has 15 teams divided into three divisions.

>>> Embiid dunks the ball in a 2017 game against the Toronto Raptors.

CHAPTER 4
MAKING HISTORY

In the 2018–2019 season, Embiid became the seventh player in the NBA to score 2,000 points, 1,000 rebounds, and 200 blocks in their first 100 games. He helped lead his team to the Eastern Conference semifinals.

In the 2019–2020 season, Embiid's average points per game dropped from 27.5 points to 23. In the playoffs, he averaged 30 points, but the 76ers lost to the Celtics.

In the 2020–2021 season, Embiid helped lead his team to become the top **seed** in the Eastern Conference for the first time in 20 years. His average points per game bounced back to 28.5. He was second in Most Valuable Player (MVP) voting for the season.

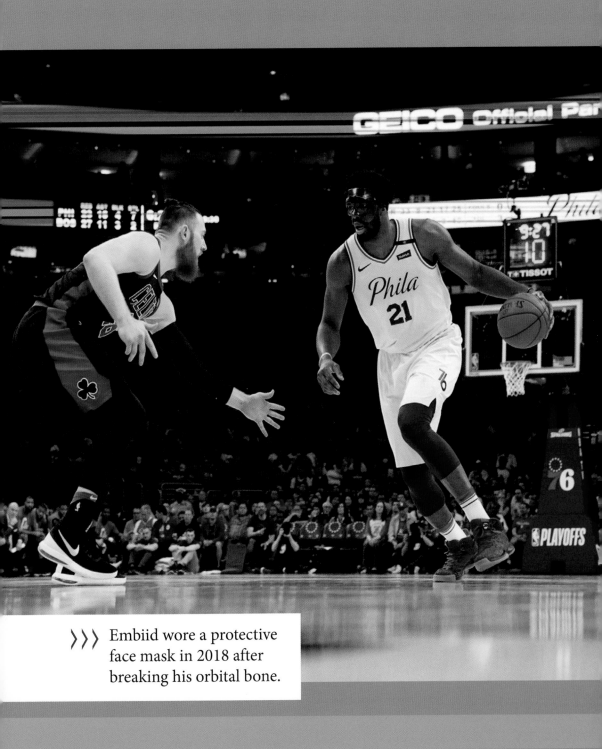

>>> Embiid wore a protective face mask in 2018 after breaking his orbital bone.

In the 2021–2022 season, Embiid missed nine games after becoming ill with COVID-19. In his return game, Embiid scored 42 points, his highest number yet in a season. Embiid struggled in his next two games as his body continued to recover.

Once he returned to full health, Embiid continued his great play. He scored more than 30 points in eight straight games. Embiid also had a long streak of games where he scored more than 25 points. In February 2022, the streak ended at 23 in a row.

>>> Embiid reaches for the ball during the tip-off in a 2021 playoff game against the Atlanta Hawks.

Embiid's hard work continued to pay off. He was named a starter in the NBA All-Star Game for the fifth year in a row. In early 2022, he was averaging more than 30 points per game. Embiid shared that he worked hard to improve his shots and passes.

Embiid hopes to continue playing for Philadelphia for the rest of his career. "This is where I want to be," said Embiid. "I want to be able to make it happen and reward the city and the fans for the trust they had in me, especially after missing two years and . . . for the trust that they've had in this process."

》》》 Embiid threw his shirt to fans after the 76ers won a 2021 playoff game against the Washington Wizards.

⟩⟩⟩ Embiid defends during
the 2018 All-Star Game.

NBA All-Star Game

The NBA All-Star Game is a yearly **exhibition** game
in February. The game showcases 24 star players in the
league. Players are selected by votes from the media,
fans, and players. Embiid joined as a starter for the 2018
All-Star Game. He was the first Philadelphia All-Star
starter since 2009. Embiid has been named to all five
All-Star games since his NBA debut.

CHAPTER 5

BEYOND THE COURT

Embiid makes a positive impact off the court. He donated his 2021 All-Star Game winnings to various homeless shelters in Philadelphia. He also partnered with the United Nations Children's Fund (UNICEF) to form the Arthur Embiid & Angels Foundation. The organization helps youth in Cameroon with education, athletics, health, and wellness. Embiid has also helped build new homes for people in Africa.

In 2018, Embiid signed an **endorsement** deal with Under Armour that extends beyond shoes and clothes. Under Armour committed to donating profits to charities in Philadelphia and Cameroon. "Basketball has given me everything, but it has to be bigger than basketball," said Embiid. "I want to use this partnership to do something real."

FACT

On September 17, 2020, Embiid became a dad to his son, Arthur, whom he named in honor of his brother.

Embiid paints a newly built house in South Africa in 2018. NBA and WNBA staff and players had volunteered to build the homes to help people in need of affordable housing.

FUTURE GOALS

Embiid wants to continue stepping forward to reach his goals. One goal is to win the MVP title. He also wants to be considered the most skilled player ever, especially for his size. However, his main goal is to work with his team to bring Philadelphia a championship title. With the way he is playing, his fans consider that a real possibility.

>>> Embiid (right) and Tobias Harris celebrate a success during a 2021 game.

TIMELINE

1994   Joel Hans Embiid is born on March 16 in Yaoundé, Cameroon.

2011   Embiid attends a Basketball Without Borders camp. Afterward, he receives a high school basketball scholarship.

2012   Embiid leads his high school team to the state championship.

2013   Embiid starts playing basketball at the University of Kansas and is named the Big 12 Defensive Player of the Year.

2014   The Philadelphia 76ers draft Embiid.

2014-2016   Embiid misses two seasons while recovering from a foot injury.

2016   Embiid makes his NBA debut.

2018   Embiid becomes one of just seven NBA players with 2,000 points, 1,000 rebounds, and 200 blocks in their first 100 games.

2021   Embiid is the runner-up MVP for the 2020–2021 season.

2022   Embiid makes the NBA All-Star team as a starter for the fifth year in a row.

GLOSSARY

ASSIST (uh-SIST)—a pass that leads to a score by a teammate

DEBUT (DAY-byoo)—a first public appearance

DRAFT (DRAFT)—an event in which athletes are picked to join sports organizations or teams

ENDORSEMENT (in-DORS-muhnt)—the act of an athlete wearing, promoting, or using a product, often for money

EXHIBITION (ek-suh-BI-shuhn)—to put on a show to demonstrate a skill

HANDBALL (HAND-bol)—a team sport where players use their hands to throw the ball into a goal

PLAYOFFS (PLAY-awfs)—a series of games played after the regular season to decide a championship

ROOKIE (RUK-ee)—a first-year player

SCHOLARSHIP (SKOL-ur-ship)—money given to students to help pay for their education

SEED (SEED)—how a team is ranked for the playoffs

READ MORE

Fishman, Jon M. *Joel Embiid*. Minneapolis: Lerner Publishing Group, Inc., 2020.

Segal, Adam Elliott. *Basketball Now!: The Stars and Stories of the NBA*. Richmond Hill, Ontario, Canada: Firefly Books, 2019.

Storden, Thom. *Basketball's Greatest Buzzer-Beaters and Other Crunch-Time Heroics*. North Mankato, MN: Capstone, 2021.

INTERNET SITES

Jr. NBA
jr.nba.com

Kiddle: Joel Embiid Facts for Kids
kids.kiddle.co/Joel_Embiid

National Basketball Association: Joel Embiid
nba.com/player/203954

INDEX

AUTHOR BIO

Cheryl Kim is an elementary teacher from California currently teaching at an international school in Thailand. She lives in Chiang Mai with her husband Brandon and sons Nathanael and Zachary.